OLD, OLD WILLOW TREE

Vernon & Linward Campbell

Library of Congress Control Number: 2019907546

ISBN:	Softcover	978-1-9845-9036-7
	Hardcover	978-1-9845-9037-4
	EBook	978-1-9845-9038-1

Print information available on the last page.

Rev. date: 01/20/2020

To order additional copies of this book, contact:
Xlibris
0800-056-3182
www.xlibrispublishing.co.uk
Orders@ Xlibrispublishing.co.uk

OLD, OLD WILLOW TREE

Author: Vernon @ Linward Campbell
Illustrations: Stewart Campbell
Song: Vernon Campbell

OLD, OLD WILLOW TREE

This **Book** Belongs to

....

OLD,
OLD
WILLOW
TREE

Once upon a time in the land of Floss
All the children one day were lost

Mums and dads looked high and low
In the sky above and the earth below

In village, towns and all around
Not one of their children could be found.

The parents went to see the King

To tell him of this sorrowful thing.

The King with sword in hand
sat on his throne in golden armour,
and on his head his royal crown

He listened to their sorrowful story, then said.

"My subjects please don't worry."
"I will do my best to find your children in a hurry."

"To do this I will need time to plan."
"To bring your children **back to the land**"

"As long as I wear this golden crown"
"I will never let you down"

The next day bright and early
He went to see his good friend Pearley

Now Pearley was a great magician
With a long white beard and a tall yellow hat
He gave the King a friendly pat

"Why are you so early?" **Said Pearley**
The King told Pearley the sad, sad story

"Dear King, I'll do my best to find them all"
"I will go and ask my crystal ball"

The King waited a long time to hear from Pearley
Then one day Pearley did appear.

He showed the King a vision of a forest
Full of wonderful singing birds

"Trees and birds are all I see"
"What of the children who are missing"

"Good King, the answer is in the tree that sings"
"But I am afraid my crystal ball is also lost"

"Somewhere in the land of Floss"

That evening at dinner, the King did raise his hand
And spoke to his protectors of the land
"Good Knights, it's time to make a stand"

"We seek the thing that is long lost"

"It is somewhere in the land of Floss"

"Now hear me well"
"It's not for me to tell"

"The good Magician will soon be here"

"Now raise your glass and give good cheer"

With a flash and a bang and a staff in hand
Magician Pearley did appear to the gathered band

He looked at the Knights all seated around the table
And knew they were brave, willing and all very able

"Brave Knight's said he. "A crystal ball is what I seek"
"It will not be found by the faint of the heart, or by the weak"

"Be brave of heart and go you forth"

"And search in lands to the north"

To a man they promised the King
They will not rest until they find the thing
They all agreed to lose not heart
And not stop until they were winners
Then they ate up all their dinners

The King stood up and said
"Whatever it takes make no mistake"
"We will find the crystal ball, one and all"

"We will search mountain pass and knee length grass"
"Across rivers and bogs and over logs"

"If along the way we meet bad strangers"
"We will stand united and bravely

face all dangers"

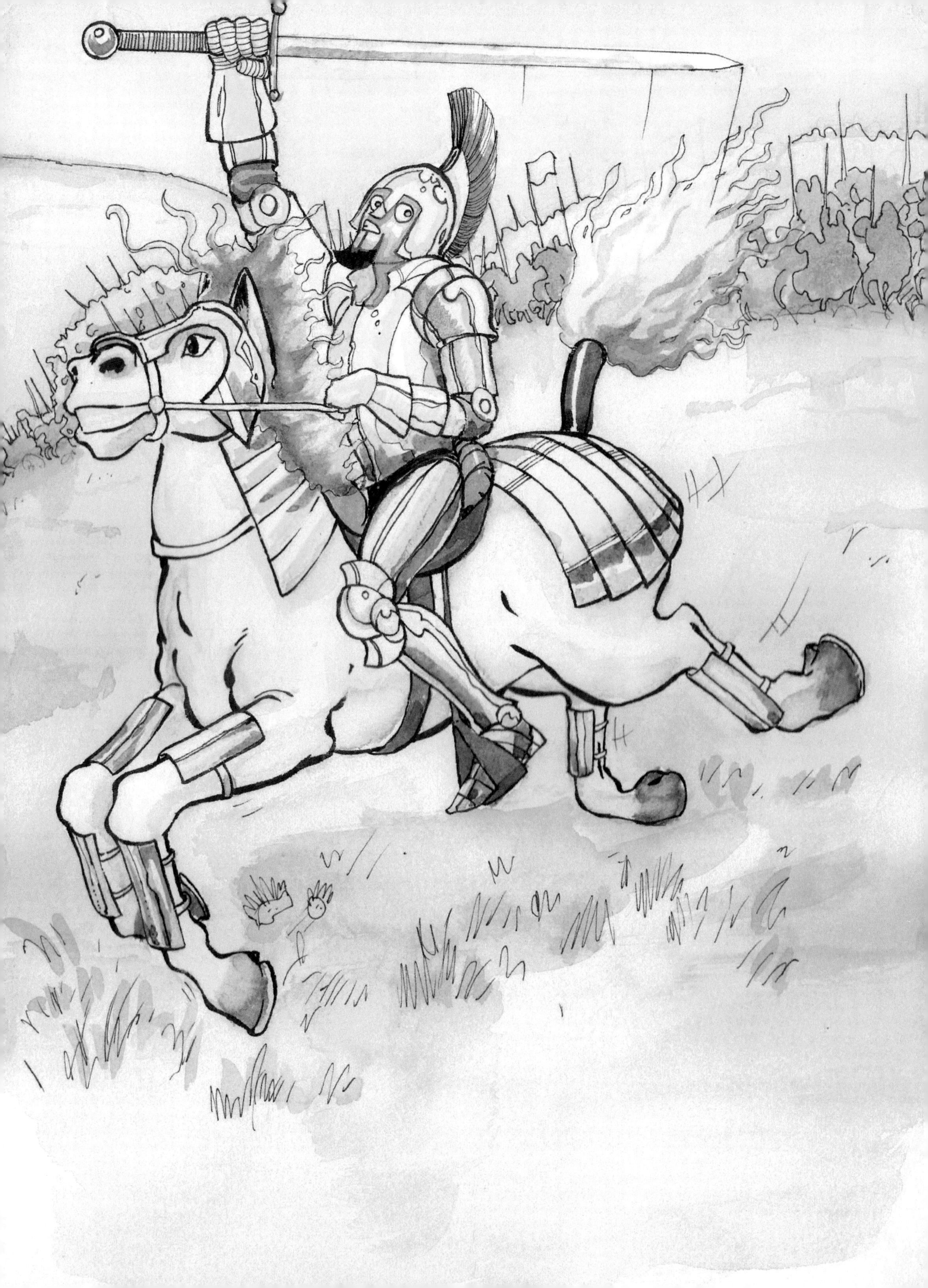

The next day at the break of dawn
The King mounted his horse called Morn

He took his place at the front of his army and said

"Good Knights, we cannot tarry"
"To find the crystal ball we must all hurry"

For months they rode through lands, always heading north
Across rivers and bogs and over logs

Their journey took them through dark places

And along the way they met many strange races

They lost their way several times throughout their journey
And near to the border they fought many Ogres

High in the mountains they faced freezing snow
And many did not know which way to go

They were frozen to the bone by snow and cold winds

And then were attacked by terrible things

A Knight named Sir Horace
and his young squire Boris
Saw a glow in a cave that was ever so dark

They were both very wise and the place they did mark

When they saw the King, they said "Hark!"

The King held high the crystal ball
And all the knights were so happy
They set off for home very snappy

The journey home wasn't so long
It was full of joyful happy songs

And all the Knights would sing along
Songs to their King, who was good and strong

The King returned the crystal ball to Pearley
Who then went straight to his place of works

There he took in hand a special wand

And chanted a ditty, that was very witty
Simple rhymes of magical words did he sing
And soon he was able to see many strange things

His song forced the crystal ball to show

The sky above and the earth below

Then he saw the tree at last
And knew he would complete his task

OLD, OLD WILLOW TREE

The next day at dawn as the sun was rising
Magician Pearley went to see the King
"Dear King, I am off to find the tree that sings"

He journeyed over land and sea

Across rivers and bogs and over logs

The journey was very slow

And Pearley had far to go

And the only way he could travel
Was on the back of a small turtle

He arrived in the forest the tree he did see
His heart was full of glee

The tree was weeping and looking quite sad
At the sight of the Magician it became very glad

"I am a weeping Willow Tree"
"I weep for all the bad things I see."

"But if you answer my riddle, I'll sing you a song"
"That will bring back the children, who are lost"
"Bring them back to the land of Floss"

"What never stand still, yet has no legs"
"It's ever so long, and so very short"

"If you lose it, you can never recover"
"And once it's gone shall never return"

"Not even for a King wearing a crown"

The Magician thought hard and long
At first, he thought it was a song

"What could it be, said he. "Does anyone know?"
He frowned and fretted, and wrinkled his brow

He walked around the old willow tree
The answer was nowhere to be seen

Then it came to him in a flash
"The answer to your riddle is, *Time*"

"It's time for you to sing, time to bring the
children back who are lost"
"Sing them back to the wonderful land of Floss"

OLD,
OLD
WILLOW
TREE

"You're right"
Said the tree and started to sing.
A song so sweet and wonderful

It was heard throughout the Land of Floss
Heard by all the children who were lost

Across time and space
Heard by all human race
Its sweet melody brought all the children back
Brought them back to the Land of Floss

Now *Mums* and *Dads* please remember this song
Sing with your children and teach them the *Words*

*For they are the most precious
treasures of all*

THE OLD, OLD WILLOW TREE SONG

1ˢᵗ Verse:

Come stormy weather, I will give you shelter
From the rays of the burning sun
I will give you cover and flourish with love,
I'm an Old, Old Willow Tree

Bridge

Fly to me, fly to me little bluebird flap your wings,
You can make your nest and lay your eggs in peace.

Chorus

I'm an old, old willow tree, an old, old willow tree,
An old, old willow tree, fly to me, fly to me
Little Bluebird Flap Your Wings

2ⁿᵈ Verse:

Little children gather hands in hand
All gods creatures great and small
Bees and the pretty painted butterflies
Nightingales in harmony, help me sing this lullaby
I'm An Old, Old Willow Tree

Bridge
Chorus

3ʳᵈ Verse:

Like veins in the body that flows through life from the roots
I fed and I grew strong now we can all sing this brand new song.
I'm An Old, Old Willow Tree

Bridge
Chorus

Printed in the United States
By Bookmasters